Clever Critters

SLIME SUPERSTARS!

By Tracy Vonder Brink

TABLE OF CONTENTS

A Crabtree Seedlings Book

Crabtree Publishing

crabtreebooks.com

School-to-Home Support for Caregivers and Teachers

This book helps children grow by letting them practice reading. Here are a few guiding questions to help readers build comprehension skills. Possible answers appear here in red.

Before Reading:

- What do I know about this topic?
    - *I know that some animals have slimy skin.*
    - *I know that some animals use slime to escape predators.*
- What do I want to learn about this topic?
    - *I want to learn which animals use slime.*
    - *I want to learn how slime is helpful.*

During Reading:

- What have I learned so far?
    - *I have learned that using slime is an adaptation.*
    - *I have learned that adaptations help living things survive.*
- I wonder why...
    - *I wonder why flies eat the slime from stinkhorn mushrooms.*
    - *I wonder why slugs climb trees.*

After Reading:

- What did I learn about this topic?
    - *I have learned that a velvet worm uses slime to hunt.*
    - *I have learned that my nose makes mucus to trap dust and germs.*
- Read the book again and look for the glossary words.
    - *I see the word **survive** on page 3 and the word **predator** on page 10. The other glossary words are found on pages 22 and 23.*

Slime made by living things is sometimes also called mucus.

SLIME SUPERSTARS!

An **adaptation** is something that helps a living thing **survive**.

Producing and using slime is one adaptation.

These animals and plants are slime superstars!

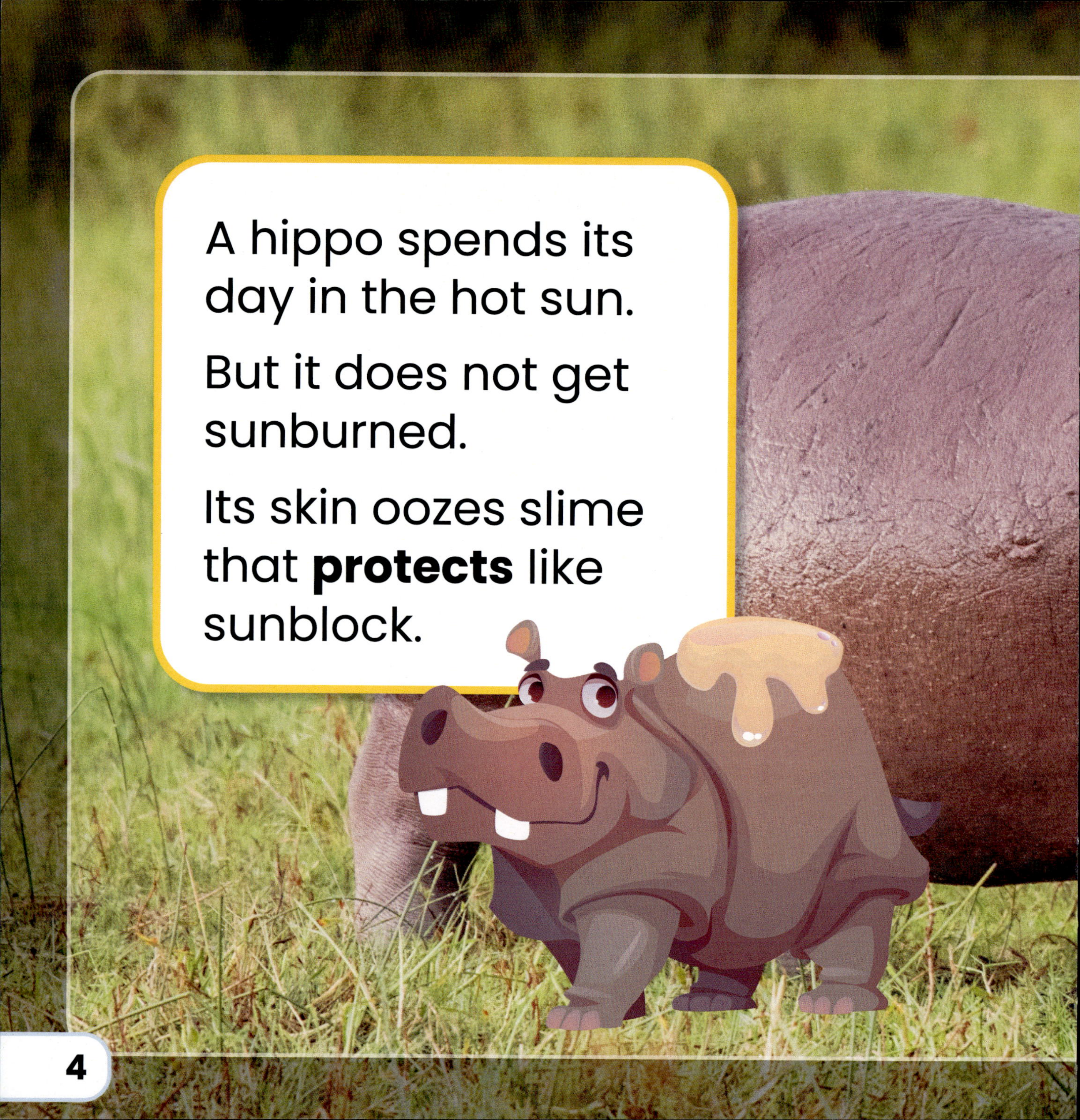

A hippo spends its day in the hot sun.

But it does not get sunburned.

Its skin oozes slime that **protects** like sunblock.

A sea sponge pulls in water through tiny holes in its body to collect **nutrients**.

But bits of sand also come with the water.

The sea sponge traps the sandy bits in slimy mucus and sneezes them out.

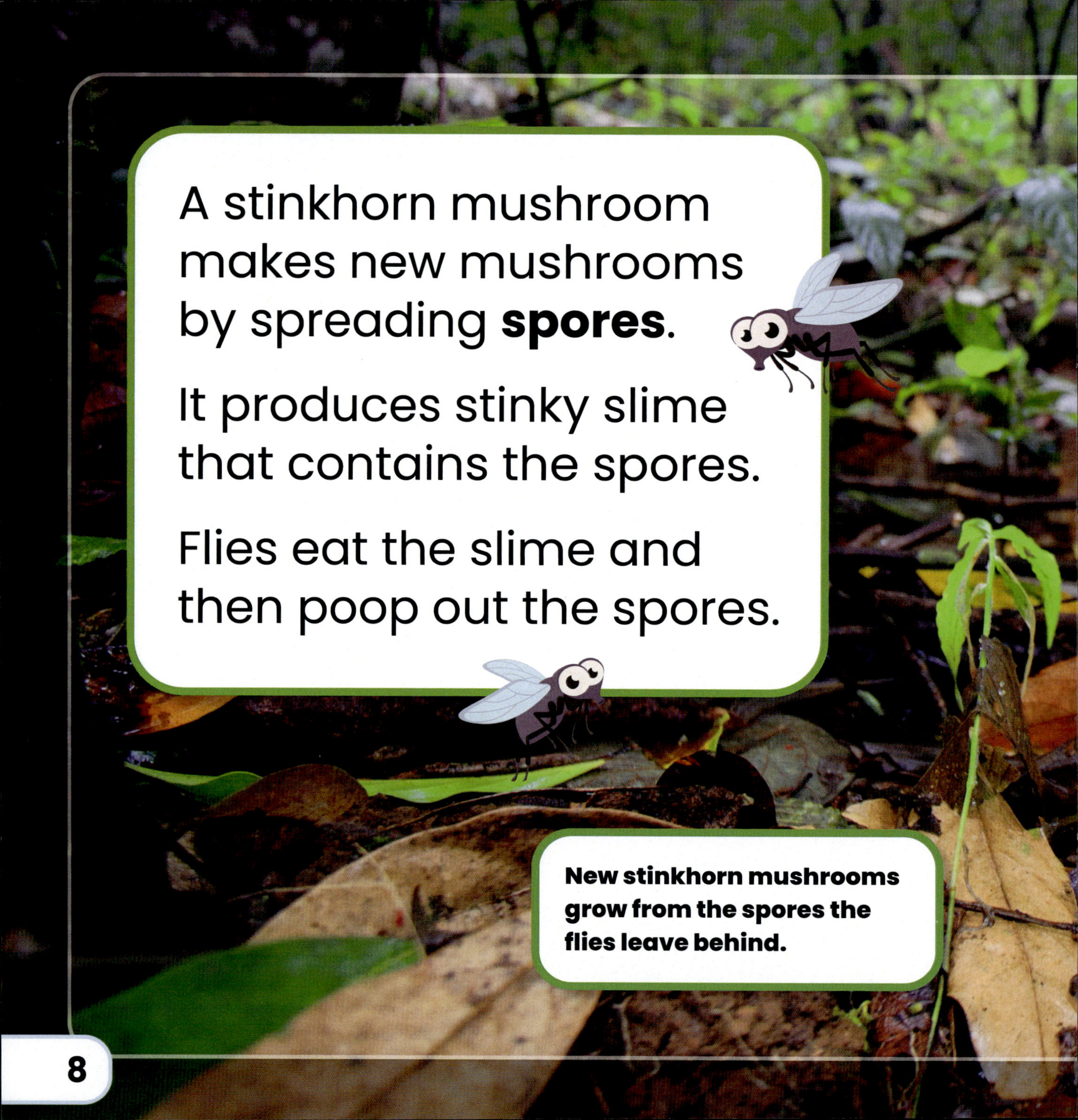

A stinkhorn mushroom makes new mushrooms by spreading **spores**.

It produces stinky slime that contains the spores.

Flies eat the slime and then poop out the spores.

New stinkhorn mushrooms grow from the spores the flies leave behind.

An octopus swims away from a hungry **predator**.

The octopus spews a dark ink cloud made of mucus.

The ink cloud scares the predator.

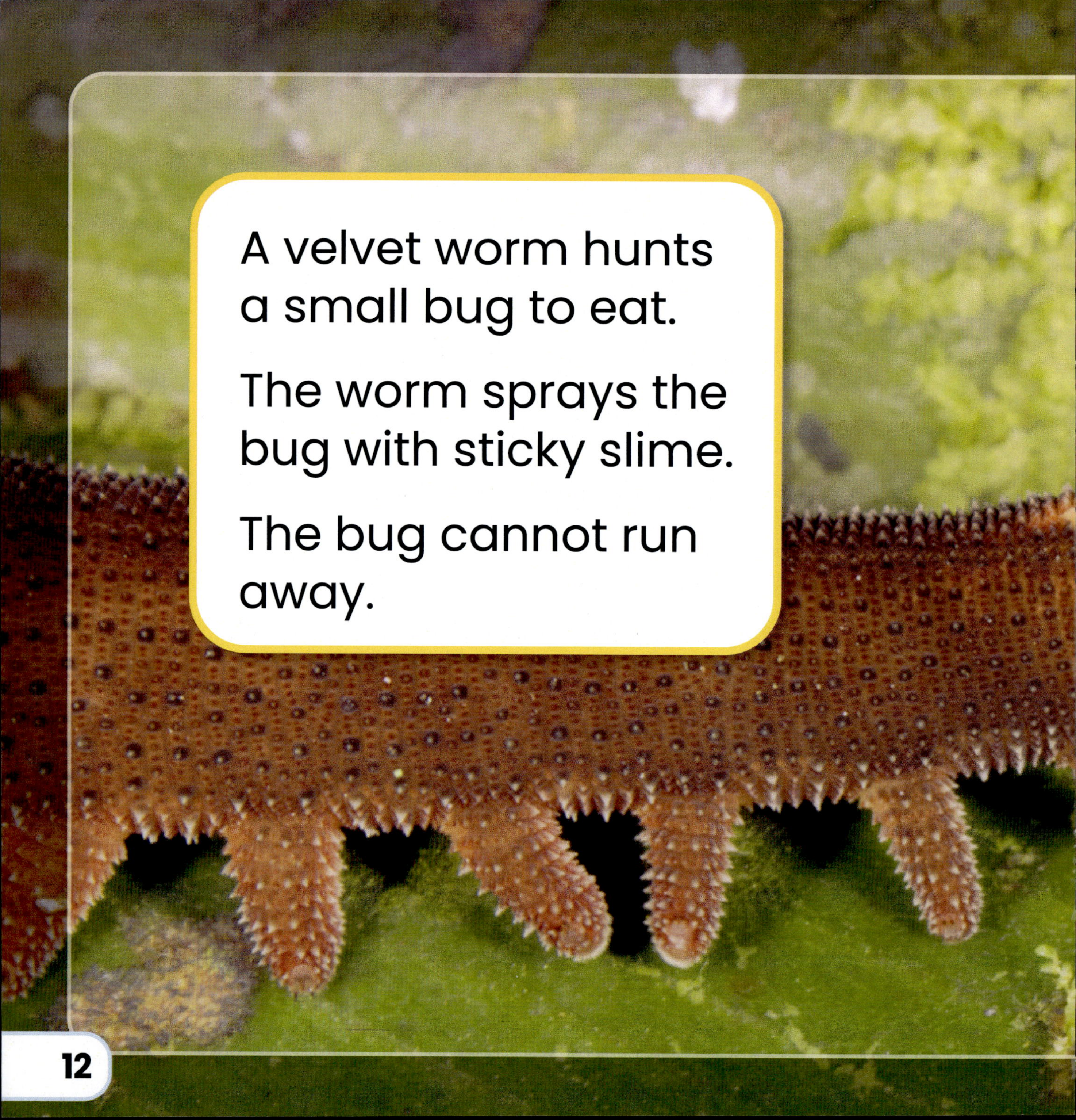

A velvet worm hunts a small bug to eat.

The worm sprays the bug with sticky slime.

The bug cannot run away.

A parrotfish uses slime to protect itself from pests that like to bite while it sleeps.

The fish makes a bubble of mucus around its body.

Pests cannot get through.

A slug climbs a tree.

As it climbs, the slug produces a layer of slime.

The slime sticks like glue so the slug does not fall.

A violet snail lives in the ocean.

It makes slimy bubbles.

It cannot swim, so it uses the bubbles to float on the ocean.

Violet snails float upside down in the water.

You need to get rid of dust and germs caught by mucus in your nose.

You sneeze to blow out the mucus.

Slime is a helpful adaptation for many living things!

Glossary

adaptation (ad-uhp-TEY-shuhn): A change in an animal or a plant that helps it live in a certain place

nutrients (NOO-tree-uhnts): Substances that people, animals, and plants need to grow and live

predator (PRED-uh-ter): An animal that lives by hunting and eating other animals

producing (pruh-DOOS-ing): Creating or making something through a natural process

protects (pruh-TEKTS): Keeps safe

spores (spohrz): Cells made by some plants that are like seeds and can grow into new plants

survive (ser-VAHYV): To continue to live

Index

About the Author

Tracy Vonder Brink loves to learn about science and nature. She has written more than 100 nonfiction books for kids. Tracy lives in Cincinnati, Ohio, with her husband, two daughters, and two rescue dogs.

Written by: Tracy Vonder Brink
Designed by: Margaret Salter
Proofreader: Melissa Boyce
Photographs: All images from Shutterstock

Crabtree Publishing

crabtreebooks.com 800-387-7650

Printed in the U.S.A./CP2025

Published in Canada
Crabtree Publishing
616 Welland Avenue
St. Catharines, Ontario
L2M 5V6

Published in the United States
Crabtree Publishing
347 Fifth Avenue
Suite 1402-145
New York, New York, 10016

Library and Archives Canada Cataloguing in Publication
Available at Library and Archives Canada

Library of Congress Cataloging-in-Publication Data
Available at the Library of Congress

Hardcover: 978-1-0398-8114-3
Paperback: 978-1-0398-8475-5
Ebook (pdf): 978-1-0398-8234-8
Epub: 978-1-0398-8354-3
Read-Along: 978-1-0398-8559-2
Audio: 978-1-0398-8517-2